Caught

A late birthday present for Nia, J.P. with T.O.L. from The Old Aunt.
x

Caught
Victoria Bean

Published 2011 by
Smokestack Books
PO Box 408, Middlesbrough TS5 6WA
e-mail : info@smokestack-books.co.uk
www.smokestack-books.co.uk

Caught
Victoria Bean
Copyright 2011, Victoria Bean, all rights reserved
Cover image: Amanda Vesey
Author photograph: Suzy Fox

Printed by
EPW Print & Design Ltd

ISBN 978-0-9564175-5-8
Smokestack Books gratefully
acknowledges the support of
Arts Council England

Smokestack Books is
represented by Inpress Ltd
www.inpressbooks.co.uk

'There's no justice. Just us.'
Graffiti, Courtroom No 4

For Robert & my boys Dan, Gabriel and Arthur

Contents

- 11 Oh oh
- 11 Previous
- 12 Hutu power
- 12 I swear
- 13 The enforcer
- 13 Court will adjourn until after lunch
- 14 A scar pleats his forehead
- 14 All rise
- 15 He bites when he fights
- 15 Hue
- 16 Not here
- 16 The prosecution exposes
- 17 A bit of luck
- 17 Boy with a knife
- 18 Not here
- 18 It ain't the first time he done it
- 19 I saw your lawyer run from the room
- 19 Hark
- 20 Can I say something else?
- 20 Feast
- 21 Same page
- 21 I have no address
- 22 Fares please
- 22 Celebration
- 23 So you say
- 23 Alias
- 24 Statement
- 24 In debt
- 25 Stand by me
- 25 Another day
- 26 The benefits of a real fire
- 26 Not guilty
- 27 From now on
- 27 What name would you like us to use?

28	It could be me
28	Holloway's your holiday
29	Skinhead
29	Just a lapse
30	Life outside
30	Pirate
31	Blue black
31	We must respect our public servants
32	Promised land
32	Extradition
33	Free meal
33	A letter from a friend & fellow member of the Buddhist Centre helps
34	Gaze
34	Public toilets/private parts
35	Not here
35	Profile of a paedophile
36	Can I say something else?
36	Fifteen years on crack
37	Not here
37	The trafficking of Miss B
38	Blonde bombshell. Black bombshell
38	Out loud
39	Lady ravens
39	Other people's words
40	Just the two of us
40	Crystal attracts an elite party crowd
41	Speak up please
41	Just a fan
42	The end of a difficult week
42	Pubic gallery
43	So I'm free now, yeah?
43	Wife beater
44	Ostraka
44	Keeping an eye out
45	30 years
45	For the girls

46 Chorus
46 I've got a confession to make
47 You are. They do.
47 Not here
48 To close my eyes
48 I'll stand if you don't mind
49 Sentence me
49 Life for another 28 days
50 Conviction
50 An international arrest warrant
51 A matter of a mile
51 A sudden loss of liberty

Oh oh

You said the f word you said the c word
you said you were on your way to Wembley
you said I'm hard, I'm hard, I could have you
you said you don't remember any of it.

Previous

Up from the cells
little Terry with an i
hands behind her back
restrained only by habit
and memory

Hutu power

Welcome to this
land of paper:

high-rise box files. Photocopy towers.

Kites of handwritten notes –

passed up, handed down.

Amid allegations of genocide
you are shown
only courtesy and justice
while a point of law gets barged at
in your defence.

You're benign now
behind glass,
behind reading glasses,
the four of you wearing cardigans
against the threat
of a November day.

I swear

I couldn't be in two places at once
he says
holding two fingers up at the judge.

The enforcer

Big, bold, erect
hair in short braids
that sprout like feelers
looking for people who owe.

When he finds you
he'll hold a kitchen knife
to your throat and
take you to a forest
in Chingford.

See that grave?
They say he said it was yours.

Court will adjourn until after lunch

She blows the kisses
he winks then waves
they exaggerate the language
to make it through the glass.

A scar pleats his forehead

Caught breaking and entering
he waves his head in disbelief
and kicks like a donkey
when bail's denied.

All rise

The church-quiet reverence
of the fixed stares and whispers in court
contradicts the Prosecutor's pencil
which is being wagged so fast
its orange paint
is now yellow.

He bites when he fights

Somewhere, on a night out in Victoria
underneath the hoardings of a Wicked
or a Billy Elliot show,
he was rude about the Irish
and bit a man twice.

Hue

The palette of this court is
grass stain green
menthol green
sixties green &
glass edge green.

Not here

Do you admit
you weren't
where
you ought
to have been?

The prosecution exposes

The prosecution leans over
revealing tight black tights
sheer from restraining
the generous white flesh
around the small black thong.

It's not been a good morning
she's already had to apologise
for her office's disarray.

A bit of luck

There's a frantic thumbs up
and a synchronised
see you downstairs
from his friend
who also needs a bath.

Boy with a knife

If you walk out of here today
arm yourself only with these words:
keep your freedom.

Keep watching those cartoons
your father says you like.

Not here

I have known Mr. Brown
in a variety of capacities
and as far as I know,
to the best of my knowledge,
he wasn't there.

It ain't the first time he done it

While the prosecutor rummages
for the statement that proves
he's done it before
his papers roar
in this room of wooden walls
and microphones.

I saw your lawyer run from the room

You want to say goodbye
but a shrug against their touch
ignites a struggle;

they kick the legs from under you
force your face into the rough carpet
squares of court

lock your hands behind your back
hold your legs, cross your feet,
and keep you there, like cattle,
until you're ready to listen.

Hark

Is that the jangle of jailer's keys
or handcuffs on the man
who nicked the bottle of wine
from an Iceland down the road?

Can I say something else?

I asked some builders
I rang Wembley police station
I spoke to the staff at the tube
I can prove all that
I won't be late again
I'll be early.

I'll sleep outside.

Feast

Stand up please.

We can't send you to jail
just because you're hungry
and it's cold outside,
however, you will stay in custody
until you've had your lunch.

Same page

The synchronized turning of pages –
flicks of white paper;
waves blanched by the wind.

The sea dies just as suddenly
when they've all found
what they're looking for.

I have no address

This is your fifth appearance,
you're becoming regular trouble
what's going wrong?

Fares please

You had to get your sick daughter from her Nan's before the post office opened, before you could get your dole.

The man from Silverlink says the one pound fifty you owe him is now one hundred and fifty pounds.

Celebration

A birthday drink.
A scrap in the street.

Break it up boys
but they just move further down the road
and do it again.

So you say

The prosecutor's scrunchie restrains
a grey brown ponytail
that explodes like bonfire smoke
on the back of a worn black suit.

The prisoner holds a wrist behind his back
already knowing
what the judge has left the room to find out.

Alias

Mr Miller is it true
you're also known
as Mr Crook?

Statement

The policeman opens his notepad to say
what would you do
if your Mrs was doing the dirty?

In debt

The judge says you can't go on owing
this sum for the rest of your life.

When did you last work? '95' she says in a whisper.

She's even lost her voice.

Stand by me

She's trying to catch your eye
even though you hid other people's
Apple Macs and Nokias
under the children's cots.

She puts her Word Search down
to record the dates of
your next court appearance.

On your way to the cells
she receives a small smile
and brief wave in return.

Another day

Another addict
another grey shirt
another chance.

The benefits of a real fire

The judge says you're on a hopeless, homeless spiral
but when you set that bin alight
you had some warmth
and for a moment

a bit of a welcoming glow.

Not guilty

No, no.   No.
No.

From now on

When you leave this dock
with your thinning apricot hair
and posture that looks like you're too tall for the room

you'll be known as
a sex offender.

What name would you like us to use?

John Clark's an opera

the deep resonance of his Irish baritone
belies his seventy year old frame

as he's led away
you can't hear the words
but you can hear the injustice
of someone betrayed by his lawyer
who's gone off to see someone 'more important than him'.

It could be me

Born on the same day, the same year,
I start looking
for anything else we have
in common.

Holloway's your holiday

Tall, tangles and a cough.

Pretty once, still only eighteen,
is anyone looking after you?

You need somewhere to stay
I sentence you to
seven days of food and sleep.

Skinhead

I am a human helicopter
flying over a landscape of
skin flaked forest floors
and number one trees,
both of us waiting
to see whether your friend gets off.

Wa hay, you say, as he does.

Just a lapse

She knows, he knows,
and now I know
because she ducks her head to laugh
every time his lawyer says
it was just a lapse.

Life outside

When you look up
there's a brief illusion
of liberty.

The giant grid of panelled lights that spans the ceiling
almost looks like sky.

Pirate

He pleads guilty to shoplifting from M&S
while a creased green carrier bag
from the same store
holding all his worldly goods
hangs between the handles of his wheelchair.

Blue black

Blue black hair
blue black coat
what's the nature
of this sexual assault?

We must respect our public servants

This was a terrible one-off incident in your life.

Aggravated assault,
hitting a cab driver,
damaging his cab,
lashing out at a policeman,
actually it was three or four things.

Promised land

I am off the drugs
oh yes,
I am off the drugs.

Extradition

The Polish man's Italian lover
shakes her head no
every time the prosecutor says yes
she will look after their children.

Free meal

Help yourself at an Angus Steak House
to a meal that costs £160.

Treat your friend –

you stayed at his flat –
and then run for it.

A letter from a friend & fellow member of the Buddhist Centre helps

This is not a simple matter
of stealing dresses to make yourself feel pretty
you're looking at custody today
there'd be no complaints if I sent you away in fact I was going to

until two minutes ago.

Gaze

We look at him looking,
rubbernecking the laptop
for one more peek
at the internet child.

Public toilets/private parts

Snap, snatch, steal
each woman recorded
by the young peeping tom
hiding with his camera.

CCTV captures him
with a more dispassionate eye.

Not here

He's refusing to attend.
He's refusing to leave his cell.

Profile of a paedophile

You're the man
we didn't notice
on the bus.

Can I say something else?

He says
I wish to say a few things.

The judge says it's usually unwise.

Fifteen years on crack

Beautiful boy
cheekbones sculpted by
sweet pink crystals still dissolving
the plump padding of his youth.

He uses car stereos as currency
but wants a second chance
for the last time,
for the hundredth time.

Not here

She appears on two wall-mounted monitors
either side of the court.

Slumped on the screen
one hand supporting her head
she would, if she could, rest her chin
on the plastic frame of one of the televisions instead.

The trafficking of Miss B

Miss B left her home in Moldavia
and came to Britain via
Germany
France
Barcelona
Malaga and then
France again.

.

Blonde bombshell. Black bombshell

Persuade the district judge, please,
that these cards,
placed in that telephone box,
will cause harassment, alarm, or distress.

Go on, say it, detective,
these scantily clad ladies, will, if you ring a certain number,
perform various sexual services.

A sexual act, performed, if you make a phone call
you keep having to say
more than once today.

Out loud

Someone's
breath
is coming
in
tidal gasps
behind
me.

Lady ravens

In hindsight there were shadows
from the bank to the market
you like off the Edgware Road.

There was a lookout, a cloak,
and the chance to spread it like an invisible wing
around your bag.

They're still watching now, this time from the dock,
the sentence unreadable on their faces,
only a muffled cry
from the hinge of the door as it closes behind them.

Other people's words

She translates
his mumbled words
and booms them back to us
with a careless inflection.

Just the two of us

He's just been released
today, yes, today, he says
into his mobile phone
in the public gallery,

and he's in court again
today, yes, today, he says
before asking his friend
if he's got any methadone.

Crystal attracts an elite party crowd

Pretty sisters used
broken glass
in ugly assault.

Speak up please

In the public gallery
I sit behind Venetian blinds
of thick vertical glass
straining to catch the softer voices
in the gaps in between.

Just a fan

He says it wasn't romantic.

The court says he broke into her agent's office
she says she never wants to hear from him again
his lawyer says he's not a danger.

His previous says he threw boiling water
over his mother.

The end of a difficult week

You shout, you swear
you cry 'food, food',
shake the charity boxes repeatedly.

You kick the door
you smash the glass
you mix rage & despair with a bottle of vodka.

Public gallery

People are still behind me
even in this empty room.

So I'm free now, yeah?

Matted hair
slipping tracksuit;
itchy blood.

Diamorphine diamond
they're not going to
punish you today.

Wife beater

He's here
because
of the things
he's seen in Iraq.

Ostraka

Muie and *Mosh* in the public gallery
with their post code surnames
gouged and scrawled
in vandals' Braille

a universal hand writes
we were here, we were here, we were here.
and names get carved in sharp angled letters
because cursive font is tricky

where the wood grain won't give.

Keeping an eye out

He's not looking around the court;
he's casing another house.

30 years

30 years a painter and decorator
'external work and snagging'
he doesn't sit on the Central Line's seats
in respect of the people
wearing suits.

For the girls

His history's all in the texts he sent:

mass immigration &
hundreds of flights on stolen credit cards,

patterns made by the telephone numbers
of flying girls into the Midlands
before sending them down to London,

Buckingham Palace Road,

and life
in a Greek Street brothel.

Chorus

The District Judge is thinking out loud

what do I do?
what do I do?
what do I do?

I've got a confession to make

Two people from work come to support her.

She's taken things from John Lewis
even though
she had enough money to buy them.

You are. They do.

When he gives his name
there are earth tremors
from a dry night in the cells.

You're an alcoholic aren't you?

Everybody who used to love you
now hates you
don't they, says the judge.

Not here

She Vaseline's her heels and then her lips
clips her nails while she waits
and then she's on –
I'm bi-polar your Honour I think I was having a breakdown
I went to my doctor
then I remembered 1.30

it just came into my head.

To close my eyes

A neighbour hears a bang,
breaking glass and more banging.

999

and the police arrive even before
the call's finished.

I was just looking for somewhere to sleep
he says when he's caught.

I'll stand if you don't mind

I don't want this man to represent me
I want to represent myself
I'll remain standing

if you don't mind.

Sentence me

The Pope's here

a good opportunity
to knick from the crowds.

The police followed you
and waited for you to do

just that.

Sentence me you say.

Life for another 28 days

The video link of the man accused of murder
interrupts the trafficker's extradition.

There's a relay of Italian
with an occasional 'ok'
whenever the man agrees
or comprehends.

The judge gives him another 28 days
and he walks off the screen
back to his cell for another month.

Conviction

I'm not sure he'll trouble the courts again.

The Magistrates nod in agreement;
economic nods,
nods they can't stop.

An international arrest warrant

From Trinidad and Tobago
to this court in Horseferry Road
what they really want
is to send you to Spain
even though you come from France.

A matter of a mile

Right, let's see
if you were,
as you say, a minute away.

The A to Z says
you were cutting it fine
your curfew's at nine.

A sudden loss of liberty

Goodbye son.
Be a good boy son.